UNOFFICIAL GUIDES

Super Smash Bros.

Beginner's Guide

21st Century Skills **INNOVATION LIBRARY**

Josh Gregory

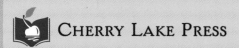
CHERRY LAKE PRESS

Published in the United States of America by Cherry Lake Publishing Group
Ann Arbor, Michigan
www.cherrylakepublishing.com

Reading Adviser: Beth Walker Gambro, MS, Ed., Reading Consultant, Yorkville, IL

Photo Credits: ©Ismail Sadiron Pictures / Shutterstock, 7; ©Natsia27 / Shutterstock, 9; ©v74 / Shutterstock, 25; ©Leonel Calara / Shutterstock, 29

Cherry Lake Press is an imprint of Cherry Lake Publishing Group.

Library of Congress Cataloging-in-Publication Data

Names: Gregory, Josh, author.
Title: Super Smash Bros. : beginner's guide / by Josh Gregory.
Description: Ann Arbor, Michigan : Cherry Lake Publishing, 2022. | Series:
   Unofficial guides | Includes bibliographical references and index. |
   Audience: Grades 4-6 | Summary: "In the wildly successful Super Smash
   Bros. series, players can choose from dozens of the most popular
   Nintendo characters as they compete in chaotic brawls. With the tips and
   strategies in this book, readers will have no trouble besting the
   competition online or in person. With Includes table of contents, author
   biography, sidebars, glossary, index, and informative backmatter"—
   Provided by publisher.
Identifiers: LCCN 2021042763 (print) | LCCN 2021042764 (ebook) | ISBN
   9781534199712 (library binding) | ISBN 9781668900857 (paperback) | ISBN
   9781668902295 (ebook) | ISBN 9781668906613 (pdf)
Subjects: LCSH: Super Smash Bros. (Game)—Juvenile literature.
Classification: LCC GV1469.35.S98 G74 2022 (print) | LCC GV1469.35.S98
   (ebook) | DDC 794.8—dc23
LC record available at https://lccn.loc.gov/2021042763
LC ebook record available at https://lccn.loc.gov/2021042764

Cherry Lake Publishing Group would like to acknowledge the work of the Partnership for 21st Century Learning, a Network of Battelle for Kids. Please visit http://www.battelleforkids.org/networks/p21 for more information.

Printed in the United States of America
Corporate Graphics

Josh Gregory is the author of more than 125 books for kids. He has written about everything from animals to technology to history. A graduate of the University of Missouri–Columbia, he currently lives in Chicago, Illinois.

Contents

CHAPTER 1

A Challenger Approaches

More than 20 years ago, the first *Super Smash Bros.* game was released for the Nintendo 64 (N64) game console. At first, this new game took players by surprise by placing some of Nintendo's most famous characters together in a fighting game. Mario and Luigi could face off against Link from *The Legend of Zelda* or Pikachu from *Pokémon*. Donkey Kong could battle against Samus, the hero of the *Metroid* games. It was unlike anything Nintendo had ever made before.

It was also unlike any fighting game anyone had played before. Most traditional fighting games are based around one-on-one battles where two players compete to knock each other out with attacks that decrease the opponent's health bar. In *Super Smash Bros.*, four players could battle each other at the same time. And their goal wasn't to simply decrease other players' health. Instead, each player had a counter that started at 0% and rose bit by bit toward 999% each time they got hit. The higher the number, the farther a player could be knocked back by powerful smash attacks. If a player got knocked back far enough, they would go flying off the side of the stage. This was the main goal of *Super Smash Bros.*: to knock opponents out of bounds while staying safely within the stage's boundaries.

Super Smash Bros. is a fast-paced fighting game that is completely unlike anything else.

Meet the Creator

Super Smash Bros. was created by legendary game developer Masahiro Sakurai. Sakurai found success in the video game industry at a very young age. When he was just 19 years old, he created the character Kirby. Kirby has gone on to star in dozens of Nintendo games, and the character is one of the company's best known mascots.

Sakurai has been the director of every game in the *Super Smash Bros.* series. He has also become a celebrity to *Smash Bros.* fans thanks to the detailed videos he makes showing off new characters and features in upcoming games.

Super Smash Bros. was the perfect game for groups of players to enjoy together, and the multiplayer mode made it one of the biggest hits on the N64. Since then, there has been a new *Super Smash Bros.* sequel released for just about every Nintendo game system. Every one of them has been a huge success. The main concept has always stayed the same, but each game has added more and more features to the formula. There have been new characters, new stages, and new items for characters to pick up during battles. *Super Smash Bros. Brawl* for the Nintendo Wii allowed players to battle each

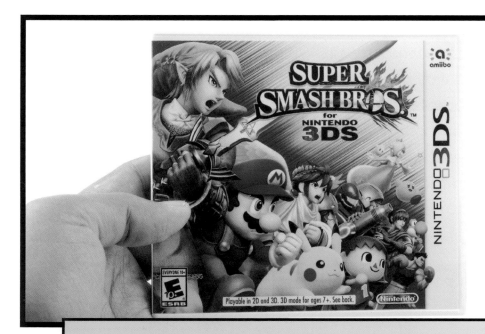

Super Smash Bros. for 3DS offered all the features and characters of *Super Smash Bros. for Wii U*, but in a portable form.

other online for the first time. *Super Smash Bros. for Wii U* doubled the number of competitors allowed in a match, allowing for hectic 8-player battles. *Super Smash Bros. for 3DS* gave players their first chance to enjoy a handheld version of the series. As the series went on, Nintendo also began including characters beyond its own popular mascots. For example, later versions have featured characters from such games as *Minecraft*, *Street Fighter*, and *Final Fantasy*.

In 2018, Nintendo announced the latest games in the series, *Super Smash Bros. Ultimate*, for Nintendo Switch. It was designed to truly be the ultimate version of the game. Every playable character that had ever been in one of the games would be included, along with several new ones. While the original *Super Smash Bros.* had featured 12 playable characters, *Ultimate* was set to feature more than 70. Longtime fans of the series went wild at the announcement.

Sonic the Hedgehog, a mascot of the Sega video game company, is one of the many non-Nintendo characters to make it into the *Super Smash Bros.* series.

While the home console and portable versions of *Super Smash Bros.* once required two separate games, *Super Smash Bros. Ultimate* offers both in one package.

It was little surprise when *Super Smash Bros. Ultimate* released to widespread acclaim. Millions of fans rushed to get copies of the game, and reviewers raved that it was the best game so far in the series. Whether you're a longtime fan or a newcomer, it's a great place to jump into the fun. If you want to compete against the best players, there's a lot you'll need to learn. The good news is that you're bound to have a lot of fun along the way.

CHAPTER 2

Joining the Battle

There are several different modes available in *Super Smash Bros. Ultimate*. Some are meant to be enjoyed as single-player experiences, while others can be enjoyed solo or in a group. The easiest way to get started is to simply select Smash from the main menu. First, you'll get to choose the settings for the match. How many lives will each player get? How long will the match last before the timer runs out? Will the winner be determined by how many knockouts a player gets, or will it simply be the last one standing. All of these rules and others can be customized. You can even adjust the difficulty level of any computer-controlled (CPU) opponents in a match or choose which items will and won't appear. Once you create a set of rules, you can save it to use again at any point in the future. You can save several different rule sets. This comes in handy if you regularly play with different groups of people who have different opinions.

Next, you can choose a stage to battle on. Each one is inspired by a famous video game. The differences between stages are much more than just looks. Some will be filled with obstacles that can be just as dangerous as attacks from your fellow fighters. Others require you to keep moving and jumping between platforms as the stage shifts through different forms.

It will take even the most dedicated players a long time to learn the ins and outs of every stage in *Super Smash Bros. Ultimate*.

Getting used to each stage will take time. If you want to simply fight on a flat, basic stage, choose Battlefield or Final Destination. These stages are designed to let players focus on combat instead of avoiding danger. If you and your fellow players can't agree on a stage, you can also let the game choose for you by picking the Random option.

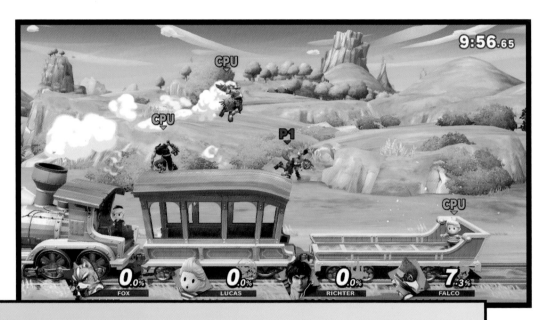

Some stages are more elaborate than others. This one takes place on a constantly moving train.

The next step is for players to choose their characters. If you are new to the game, you'll only have a few to choose from. Dozens more will be unlocked as you play. With so many options, how do you pick the right one? There is really no right answer. Some players insist that certain characters are just better than others. However, any character in the game can be used to defeat every other character if you play well. Sometimes it is just a matter of trying a strategy no one else has thought of yet. Some characters have simpler sets of moves than others. This makes them a

An Ever-Growing Game

Super Smash Bros. Ultimate was a massive game from the very beginning, with dozens of characters available. However, the game has gotten even bigger since it was released. Nintendo regularly releases new downloadable fighters, stages, and even new modes. Many of these additions can be purchased one at a time through microtransactions or bundled together as part of the larger Fighter's Pass expansions. Other times, new features are given away for free to all players. Keeping up with all the latest additions can be time-consuming (and expensive!), but it ensures that even the most dedicated players always have something new to try.

little easier for new players to learn. But the best thing to do is simply try as many characters as you can and then choose a couple of them to keep practicing with. Eventually, you might settle on a single main character that you stick with most of the time. This is how the world's top players usually approach *Super Smash Bros.* and other fighting games.

On the character selection screen, you can also choose whether or not to add CPU players to the mix. If you are playing alone, you'll need at least one CPU fighter

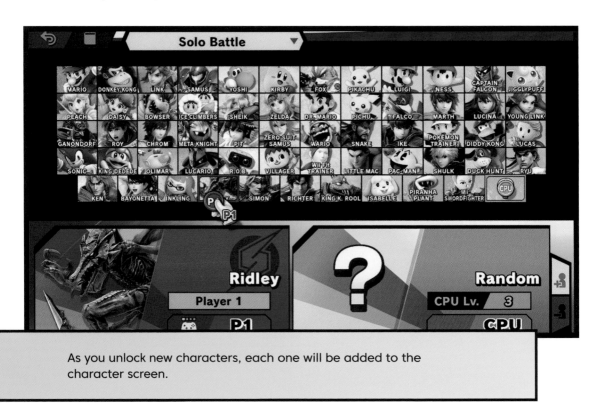

As you unlock new characters, each one will be added to the character screen.

to battle against. If you are playing with friends, you can add however many CPU players it takes to reach the maximum of 8 players. You can also leave CPU players out if you like.

No matter which mode you decide to play, the basic flow of the game will always be the same. Your goal is to damage your opponents as much as possible, then knock them out of bounds. Keep a close eye on the bottom of the screen to see each character's damage. Here, you can also see how many lives each player has in stock. This information can help you determine when to launch an attack and when to play more defensively. But even if your damage is low and another player's is high, you are not always safe. If you aren't careful, you could get knocked off a ledge when you aren't expecting it, or your opponent could make a well-timed jump back to safety after you thought you had a sure knockout.

There are many, many ways to damage your opponents in *Super Smash Bros*. Each character has a different range of moves. Playing as one fighter can be a very different experience from playing as another. However, there are a few basics that stay the same no matter who you choose to play as. For example, all

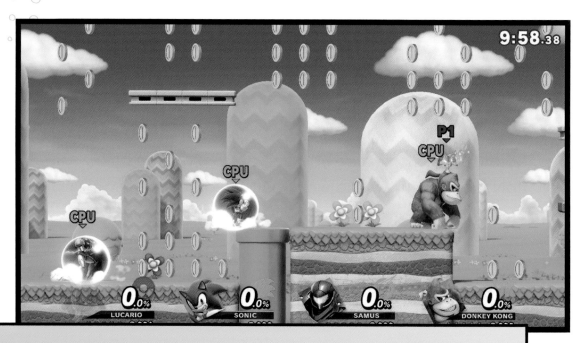

If an enemy has their shield up, try a grab attack. It can reach right through the shield.

characters can perform a set of regular attacks with the A button and special attacks with the B button. The exact attack each button produces depends on which direction you move the control stick as you press the button. Some characters' attacks also allow you to hold buttons down before releasing them to get different results.

In addition to these attacks, all characters can put up a temporary shield to block damage from incoming attacks. Do this by pressing ZR or ZL. The shield looks like a colored orb. It shrinks in size as you hold the shield button, until it disappears completely. This keeps players from simply guarding the entire time. All characters can also grab and throw opponents by pressing the L or R buttons. Hold down either the grab or shield button, then press the left control stick in different directions to perform a dodge. This is a great way to avoid incoming attacks at the last moment.

Jumping plays a very big role in *Super Smash Bros.* Press Y or X to jump. Your feet don't have to be touching the ground to do this. While you are in the air, most characters can jump up to two times before touching the ground. Many characters can also get some extra height by holding up on the left stick and pressing B to perform an upward special attack. Get a feel for your character's jump movements as soon as you can. You'll need to time them carefully to get back to safety when you get knocked off a ledge. Once you get the hang of it, you'll be bouncing all over the place during battles.

Another thing to watch out for is items. These can really turn the tide of battle. There are dozens of different ones, and they will drop into stages at random. Some are as simple as hammer or bats you can use to bash your opponents. Others have more specialized effects. For example, picking up the Bunny Hood will let your character jump higher for a limited time. A Poke Ball can be used to summon a random computer-controlled Pokémon to fight by your side. It's very helpful to learn which items work best for which

Many of the items in *Super Smash Bros.* are as funny as they are powerful. A giant flower can become a dangerous weapon!

situations. You should also pay attention to which items your opponents pick up. That way they won't catch you off guard with a surprising attack!

You already know that your attacks are different depending on which direction your character is moving. But some attacks are also affected by the speed of your movement. For example, the same attack might give you different results if you are running at full speed or if you are barely tilting

Standard attacks are useful for building up an opponent's damage to make them fly farther.

You can hold down the buttons of a smash attack to make it more powerful before releasing. As you do, you'll see a sparkle like this one.

the left stick to move. Try it out and see what happens!

When you are ready to knock a highly damaged opponent as far as possible, try a smash attack. Smash attacks can be done in two different ways. The simplest is to simply push the right stick in the direction you want to attack. The other way is to press the A button and tap the left stick in a direction at the same time. Either way, these attacks will send your opponents flying farther than most other moves. They are a great way to finish off a powerful combo.

Whether you're battling a CPU player or a fellow human, you'll want to learn to pay close attention to your opponents' behavior. Being able to read their movements and predict their next actions will help you figure out the most effective way to battle. There is no easy way to learn this skill. It takes sharp eyes and a lot of practice.

Remember that each character has different strengths and weaknesses. Some have moves that are almost entirely long-range. Others require you to get up close and personal with opponents. There are also differences beyond which moves characters can do. Some are larger and slower. Others are very fast. Some can jump farther than others. All of this means you might need to get creative depending who you are battling. If something isn't working, don't be afraid to switch up your strategy. Notice what your opponents do well and what they do poorly. Then think about your own strengths. Use this information to your advantage as often as possible!

CHAPTER 3

The Right Moves

Once you get a feel for the basics of *Super Smash Bros.*, it's time to start thinking about more advanced strategies. In such a fast-paced game, you won't have much time to stop and plan out your approach. This means you'll need to memorize the most useful techniques until they become almost automatic. At first, this might seem overwhelming. But once it clicks, it's a lot like riding a bike!

One important technique is known among fans as edge guarding. When you knock an opponent off a ledge or toward the edge of the screen, they have a chance to jump back to safety. But with the right timing and positioning, you can jump toward your enemy and knock them back in midair before they have a chance to get their feet on solid ground. This makes it very tough for them to recover if they have already jumped twice in midair. Of course, you'll also need to watch out for opponents who try to do the same thing to you.

In general, it's very important to get used to battling in midair. Any time you are in the air, you can use the left stick to move from side to side. Pressing A while holding the left stick in different directions will let you perform basic **aerial** attacks. You can also use your special B-button attacks and perform grabs like

Mastering your moves in the air is in many ways even more important than getting around on the ground in *Super Smash Bros*.

normal. Just like on the ground, getting hit will knock you back. One very useful trick to master is the air dodge. Simply press the shield button while holding the left stick in any direction to perform a quick dash in that direction. This can help you avoid attacks or help you make a safe landing.

Under Control

Each Nintendo game system has a different style of controller, from the Wii's Wiimote to the Switch's detachable Joy-Con. Additionally, many fighting game fans like to use special devices called fight sticks. These large controllers position a single joystick and all of the necessary buttons on a flat surface, much like the controls on arcade game machines.

Players have different preferences about which controllers work best for *Smash Bros.* In the end, most people are happy to play using whichever devices are easily available. But others take controllers very seriously. The GameCube controller has an especially devoted fanbase among *Smash Bros.* players. When the Wii U and Switch versions of the game were released, Nintendo even created a special adaptor that allowed players to plug their GameCube controllers into the newer systems.

Even though they are old, GameCube controllers are still many *Smash Bros.* players' favorite tools.

When you try a new character, you might find a certain move or attack that seems to work very well. However, you should avoid repeating the same move over and over again. The more you use a move, the weaker it will become. Its strength will return as you mix other moves into your attacks. This feature is designed to make players use all the tools at each character's disposal. Instead of attacking the same way repeatedly, try to build combos by stringing different moves together. For example, you might use at attack that launches your opponent into the air. Then you might jump toward them and hit them with an aerial attack. Before they hit the ground, you

Each character's attacks are often references to the other games they appear in. Luigi uses his ghost-capturing vacuum from the *Luigi's Mansion* series to grab opponents.

might grab them and throw them off the edge of the stage. To get good at this, you'll need to be very familiar with all of your character's moves. It takes a lot of practice, but a good combo is the sign of a truly skilled player.

As you get more practice, you'll find your character at the top of the victory screen more and more often.

CHAPTER 4

The Competitive Scene

Over the years, *Super Smash Bros.* has built up a huge **esports** following. As early as 2002, major tournaments were held for *Super Smash Bros. Melee*. Today, there are thousands of pro *Super Smash Bros.* events held around the world every year. The best players have earned tens of thousands of dollars playing the game. Some focus on a specific game in the series. For example. *Super Smash Bros. Melee* has remained popular as an esports title even as new games in the series have been released.

Pro *Super Smash Bros.* competitions typically use a specific set of rules that are meant to make the game as fair as possible. For example, items are usually turned off, and there are rules for determining which player gets to choose the stage for a match.

Even though *Super Smash Bros.* is very different from most fighting games, it has also found a place in the world of fighting game esports. Every year, it is one of the games featured at the Evolution Championship Series, known simply as Evo to fans. This is one of the biggest and most famous annual events in the world of fighting games. At Evo 2019, *Super Smash Bros. Ultimate* even set a record as the most-watched game in the tournament's history. More than 279,000 fans

Pro *Super Smash Bros.* players compete at an esports event in California in 2019.

tuned in to watch online, with thousands more attending in person.

Super Smash Bros. is also very popular on streaming services such as Twitch. Successful pro players often stream their practice sessions. They might also offer tutorials and explain strategies to viewers. This can be a great way to learn more about the game and gets tips for improving your own skills.

Time for Training

Want to tighten up your *Smash Bros.* skills? Check out the game's Training mode. Here, you can choose your fighter, stage, and opponent and practice moves as long as you want. If you like, you can choose the special training stage to play on a numbered grid. This will let you measure exactly how far back each of your attacks can knock an enemy. The game will also let you know how much damage you are dealing with each combo and individual attack.

If you pause the game in Training mode, you will see options for setting the computer-controlled opponent's behavior. This lets you train for specific situations. You can also access a list of every character's unique moves. This is a great way to learn how to use characters you aren't familiar with.

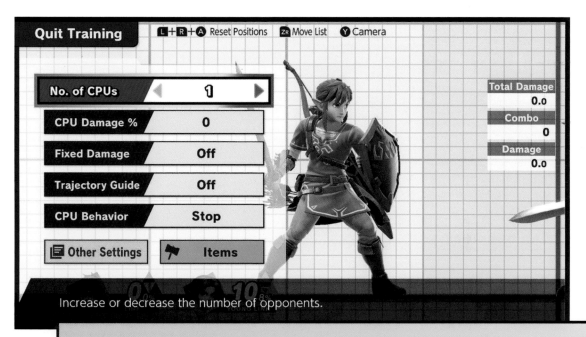

| Quit Training | L + R + A Reset Positions | ZR Move List | Y Camera |

No. of CPUs	◀ 1 ▶
CPU Damage %	0
Fixed Damage	Off
Trajectory Guide	Off
CPU Behavior	Stop
🗐 **Other Settings**	🚩 **Items**

Total Damage	0.0
Combo	0
Damage	0.0

Increase or decrease the number of opponents.

Training mode offers plenty of options for practicing the exact skills you need to improve.

Although *Super Smash Bros.* can be a very competitive experience, the most important thing is always to have a good time. Even if a match doesn't go your way, there's always next time. You'll keep getting better as you play more. Have fun!

GLOSSARY

aerial (AYR-ee-uhl) taking place in the air

developer (dih-VEL-uh-pur) someone who makes video games or other computer programs

esports (EE-sports) professional video game competitions

microtransactions (MYE-kroh-trans-ak-shuhnz) something that can be purchased for a small amount of money within a video game or other computer program

FIND OUT MORE

Books

Cunningham, Kevin. *Video Game Designer*. Ann Arbor, MI: Cherry Lake Publishing, 2016.

Loh-Hagan, Virginia. *Video Games*. Ann Arbor, MI: Cherry Lake Publishing, 2021.

Powell, Marie. *Asking Questions About Video Games*. Ann Arbor, MI: Cherry Lake Publishing, 2016.

Websites

SmashWiki, the Super Smash Bros. Wiki
https://www.ssbwiki.com/
Check out this highly detailed, fan-made guide to the Super Smash Bros. series.

Super Smash Bros. Ultimate - Official Website
https://www.smashbros.com/en_US/
Get the latest *Smash* updates from the official website.

INDEX